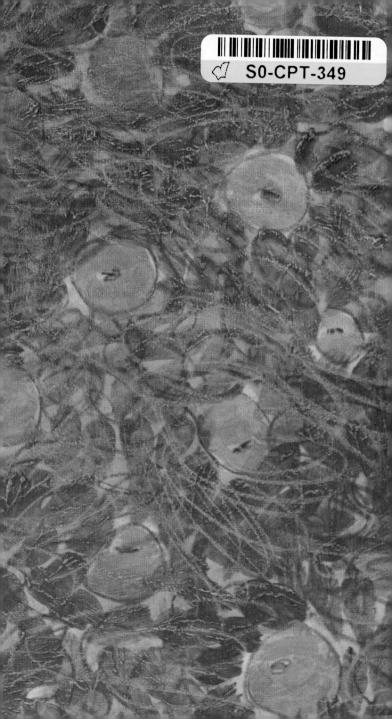

THE RUBAYYAT OF OMAR KHAYYAM

The Rubayyat of Omar Khayyam

LIFE AND LOVE
IN ONE OF THE WORLD'S
MOST FAMOUS POEMS
IN THE CLASSIC TRANSLATION
OF EDWARD FITZGERALD

With an Introduction
by Manoocher Aryanpur

Illustrated by Joseph Isom

HALLMARK EDITIONS

Edited by Gwynne Bujarsky

INTRODUCTION

When Edward FitzGerald brought out his first edition of Omar Khayyam's *Rubayyat* in 1859, no one, not even FitzGerald himself, dreamed of the fame that the 11th century Persian poet was to attain in the West. By chance, the haunting songs of a sage had crossed the cultural and linguistic bounds that confined him to a relatively limited audience for centuries. Fitz-Gerald intended to make the voice heard in the English-speaking world. The English language, he felt, would provide the necessary range for the songs to take wing.

For a time it seemed as though the *Rubayyat* was to become another of FitzGerald's failures. During the first two years, only a few copies were sold at the regular price of three shillings, and the English *Rubayyat* appeared doomed. Indeed, to get rid of the unsold copies, the publisher relegated them to a stall in St. Martin's Lane where they were to be disposed of at a penny each.

Then a miracle occurred. Algernon Charles Swinburne and Dante Gabriel Rossetti, the two famous poets, bought the *Rubayyat* and were entranced by it. As they publicized their discovery, there developed an ever-increasing demand for the book, and the exotic Khayyam's fame began to spread.

In less than two decades, the *Rubayyat* was translated into 17 languages and several million copies of the book were sold all over the world. Thus it was that Omar Khayyam, for centuries unknown outside of the Middle East, took his place among the literary giants of the world.

Khayyam's initial popularity might have had something to do with chance as well as with the exotic flavor of his poetry. To an age attracted by the bizarre, his poetry in its gorgeous Victorian garb was as interesting as Toulouse-Lautrec, Chinese dolls, or Oscar Wilde. But the steady popularity of the book in the last 100 years makes it clear that the *Rubayyat* offers more than fad or novelty.

To discover the secret of Omar Khayyam's charm, one must go to the *Rubayyat* itself; particularly since, aside from a few legends, next to nothing is known of the man. It is in the *Rubayyat* alone that the solitary figure of the poet shines through. We can watch him make his rounds to his library, his tavern, his mistress, a potter's shop, an owl-haunted caravansary, and finally a tomb. And if thus following the sage, we desire to know more about his ideas, we must harken to his own words.

Manoocher Aryanpur

THE RUBAYYAT OF OMAR KHAYYAM

AWAKE! for Morning in the Bowl of Night

Has flung the Stone that puts the Stars to Flight:

And Lo! the Hunter of the East has caught

The Sultan's Turret in a Noose of Light.

Dreaming when Dawn's Left Hand was in the Sky

I heard a voice within the Tavern cry,

"Awake, my Little ones, and fill the Cup

Before Life's Liquor in its Cup be dry."

III

And, as the Cock crew, those who stood before

The Tavern shouted—"Open then the Door!

You know how little while we have to stay,

And, once departed, may return no more."

IV

Now the New Year reviving old Desires,

The thoughtful Soul to Solitude retires,

Where the White Hand of Moses on the Bough

Puts out, and Jesus from the Ground suspires.

V

Iram indeed is gone with all its Rose,

And Jamshyd's Sev'n-ring'd Cup where no one Knows;

But still the Vine her ancient ruby yields,

And still a Garden by the Water blows.

VI

And David's Lips are lock't; but in divine

High piping Pehlevi, with "Wine! Wine! Wine!

Red Wine!" — the Nightingale cries to the Rose

That yellow Cheek of hers to incarnadine.

VII

Come, fill the Cup, and in the Fire of Spring

The Winter Garment of Repentance fling:

The Bird of Time has but a little way

To fly—and Lo! the Bird is on the Wing.

VIII

Whether at Naishapur or Babylon,

Whether the Cup with sweet or bitter run,

The Wine of Life keeps oozing drop by drop,

The Leaves of Life keep falling one by one.

Morning a thousand Roses brings, you say;

Yes, but where leaves the Rose of Yesterday?

And this first Summer month that brings the Rose

Shall take Jamshyd and Kaikobad away.

But come with old Khayyam, and leave the Lot

Of Kaikobad and Kaikhosru forgot:

Let Rustum lay about him as he will,

Or Hatim Tai cry Supper—heed them not.

With me along the strip of Herbage strown

That just divides the desert from the sown,

Where name of Slave and Sultan is forgot—

And Peace is Mahmud on his Golden Throne!

A Book of Verses underneath the Bough,

A Jug of Wine, a Loaf of Bread,—and Thou

Beside me singing in the Wilderness—

Oh, Wilderness were Paradise enow!

XIII

Some for the Glories of This World; and some

Sigh for the Prophet's Paradise to come;

Ah, take the Cash, and let the Promise go,

Nor heed the rumble of a distant Drum!

XIV

Were it not Folly, Spider-like to spin

The Thread of present Life away to win—

What? for ourselves, who know not if we shall

Breathe out the very Breath we now breathe in!

Look to the Rose that blows about us—"Lo,

Laughing," she says, "into the World I blow:

At once the silken Tassel of my Purse

Tear, and its Treasure on the Garden throw."

The Worldly Hope men set their Hearts upon

Turns Ashes—or it prospers; and anon,

Like Snow upon the Desert's dusty Face

Lighting a little Hour or two—is gone.

XVII

And those who husbanded the Golden Grain,

And those who flung it to the Winds like Rain,

Alike to no such aureate Earth are turn'd

As, buried once, Men want dug up again.

XVIII

Think, in this batter'd Caravanserai

Whose Doorways are alternate Night and Day,

How Sultan after Sultan with his Pomp

Abode his Hour or two and went his way.

They say the Lion and the Lizard keep

The Courts where Jamshyd gloried and drank deep:

And Bahram, that great Hunter—the Wild Ass

Stamps o'er his Head, but cannot break his Sleep.

XX

I sometimes think that never blows so red

The Rose as where some buried Caesar bled;

That every Hyacinth the Garden wears

Dropt in its Lap from some once lovely Head.

And this delightful Herb whose tender Green

Fledges the River's Lip on which we lean —

Ah, lean upon it lightly! for who knows

From what once lovely Lip it springs unseen!

XXII

Ah, my Beloved, fill the Cup that clears

To-day of past Regrets and future Fears —

To-morrow? — Why, To-morrow I may be

Myself with Yesterday's Sev'n Thousand Years.

XXIII

Lo! some we loved, the loveliest and best

That Time and Fate of all their Vintage prest,

Have drunk their Cup a Round or two before,

And one by one crept silently to Rest.

XXIV

And we, that now make merry in the Room

They left, and Summer dresses in new Bloom,

Ourselves must we beneath the Couch of Earth

Descend, ourselves to make a Couch — for whom?

XXV

Ah, make the most of what we may yet spend,

Before we too into the Dust descend;

Dust into Dust, and under Dust, to lie,

Sans Wine, sans Song, sans Singer, and—sans End!

XXVI

Alike for those who for To-day prepare,

And those that after some To-morrow stare,

A Muezzin from the Tower of Darkness cries

"Fools! Your Reward is neither Here nor There!"

XXVII

Why, all the Saints and Sages who discuss'd

Of the Two Worlds so learnedly, are thrust

Like foolish Prophets forth; their Works to Scorn

Are scatter'd, and their Mouths are stopt with Dust.

XXVIII

Oh, come with old Khayyam, and leave the Wise

To talk; one thing is certain, that Life flies;

One thing is certain, and the Rest is Lies;

The Flower that once has blown forever dies.

XXIX

Myself when young did eagerly frequent

Doctor and Saint, and heard great Argument

About it and about; but evermore

Came out by the same Door as in I went.

XXX

With them the Seed of Wisdom did I sow,

And with my own hand labour'd it to grow:

And this was all the Harvest that I reap'd—

"I came like Water and like Wind I go."

Into this Universe, and Why not knowing,

Nor Whence, like Water willy-nilly flowing:

And out of it, as Wind along the Waste,

I know not Whither, willy-nilly blowing.

Up from Earth's Centre through the Seventh Gate

I rose, and on the Throne of Saturn sate,

And many Knots unravel'd by the Road;

But not the Master-Knot of Human Fate.

XXXIII

There was the Door to which I found no Key:

There was the Veil through which I could not see:

Some little talk awhile of Me and Thee

There was—and then no more of Thee and Me.

XXXIV

Then to the rolling Heav'n itself I cried,

Asking, "What Lamp had Destiny to guide

Her little Children stumbling in the Dark?"

And—"A blind Understanding!" Heav'n replied.

XXXV

Then to the Lip of this poor earthen Urn

I lean'd, the secret Well of Life to learn:

And Lip to Lip it murmur'd—"While you live,

Drink!—for, once dead, you never shall return."

XXXVI

I think the Vessel, that with fugitive

Articulation answer'd, once did live,

And merry-make, and the cold Lip I kiss'd,

How many Kisses might it take—and give!

28

XXXVII

For in the Market-place, one Dusk of Day,

I watch'd the Potter thumping his wet Clay:

And with its all obliterated Tongue

It murmur'd—"Gently, Brother, gently, pray!"

XXXVIII

And has not such a Story from of Old

Down Man's successive generations roll'd

Of such a clod of saturated Earth

Cast by the Maker into Human mould?

Ah, fill the Cup: — what boots it to repeat

How Time is slipping underneath our Feet:

Unborn To-morrow, and dead Yesterday,

Why fret about them if To-day be sweet!

XL

A Moment's Halt — a momentary taste

Of Being from the Well amid the Waste —

And Lo! the phantom Caravan has reach'd

The Nothing it set out from — Oh, make haste!

Oh, plagued no more with Human or Divine,

To-morrow's tangle to itself resign,

And lose your fingers in the tresses of

The Cypress-slender Minister of Wine.

Waste not your Hour, nor in the vain pursuit

Of This and That endeavor and dispute;

Better be merry with the fruitful Grape

Than sadden after none, or bitter, fruit.

You know, my Friends, with what a brave Carouse

I made a Second Marriage in my house;

Divorced old barren Reason from my Bed,

And took the Daughter of the Vine to Spouse.

XLIV

And lately, by the Tavern Door agape,

Came stealing through the Dusk an Angel Shape

Bearing a Vessel on his Shoulder; and

He bid me taste of it; and 'twas — the Grape!

The Grape that can with Logic absolute

The Two-and-Seventy jarring Sects confute:

The subtle Alchemist that in a Trice

Life's leaden Metal into Gold transmute.

XLVI

Why, be this Juice the growth of God, who dare

Blaspheme the twisted tendril as a Snare?

A Blessing, we should use it, should we not?

And if a Curse — why, then, Who set it there?

But leave the Wise to wrangle, and with me

The Quarrel of the Universe let be:

And, in some corner of the Hubbub couch'd,

Make Game of that which makes as much of Thee.

XLVIII

For in and out, above, about, below,

'Tis nothing but a Magic Shadow-show,

Play'd in a Box whose Candle is the Sun,

Round which we Phantom Figures come and go.

XLIX

Strange, is it not? that of the myriads who

Before us pass'd the door of Darkness through

Not one returns to tell us of the Road,

Which to discover we must travel too.

L

The Revelations of Devout and Learn'd

Who rose before us, and as Prophets burn'd,

Are all but Stories, which, awoke from Sleep,

They told their fellows, and to Sleep return'd.

Why, if the Soul can fling the Dust aside,

And naked on the Air of Heaven ride,

Is't not a shame—Is't not a shame for him

So long in this Clay suburb to abide?

But that is but a Tent wherein may rest

A Sultan to the realm of Death addrest;

The Sultan rises, and the dark Ferrash

Strikes, and prepares it for another guest.

LIII

I sent my Soul through the Invisible,

Some letter of that After-life to spell:

And after many days my Soul return'd

And said, "Behold, Myself am Heav'n and Hell."

LIV

Heav'n but the Vision of fulfill'd Desire,

And Hell the Shadow of a Soul on fire,

Cast on the Darkness into which Ourselves,

So late emerg'd from, shall so soon expire.

While the Rose blows along the River Brink,

With old Khayyam and ruby vintage drink:

And when the Angel with his darker Draught

Draws up to Thee—take that, and do not shrink.

And fear not lest Existence closing your

Account, should lose, or know the type no more;

The Eternal Saki from the Bowl has pour'd

Millions of Bubbles like us, and will pour.

LVII

When You and I behind the Veil are past,

Oh but the long long while the World shall last,

Which of our Coming and Departure heeds

As much as Ocean of a pebble-cast.

LVIII

'Tis all a Chequer-board of Nights and Days

Where Destiny with Men for Pieces plays:

Hither and thither moves, and mates, and slays,

And one by one back in the Closet lays.

LIX

The Ball no Question makes of Ayes and Noes,

But Right or Left, as strikes the Player goes;

And He that toss'd Thee down into the Field,

He knows about it all—He knows—HE knows!

LX

The Moving Finger writes; and, having writ,

Moves on: nor all thy Piety nor Wit

Shall lure it back to cancel half a Line,

Nor all thy Tears wash out a Word of it.

For let Philosopher and Doctor preach

Of what they will, and what they will not—each

Is but one Link in an eternal Chain

That none can slip, nor break, nor over-reach.

LXII

And that inverted Bowl we call The Sky,

Whereund   ling coop't we live and die,

Lift not thy hands to It for help—for It

Rolls impotently on as Thou or I.

With Earth's first Clay They did the Last Man knead,

And then of the Last Harvest sow'd the Seed:

Yea, the first Morning of Creation wrote

What the Last Dawn of Reckoning shall read.

LXIV

Yesterday This Day's Madness did prepare;

To-morrow's Silence, Triumph, or Despair:

Drink! for you know not whence you came, nor why:

Drink! for you know not why you go, nor where.

LXV

I tell You this—When, starting from the Goal,

Over the shoulders of the flaming Foal

Of Heav'n Parwin and Mushtari they flung,

In my predestin'd Plot of Dust and Soul.

LXVI

The Vine has struck a fiber: which about

If clings my Being—let the Dervish flout;

Of my Base metal may be filed a Key,

That shall unlock the Door he howls without.

And this I know: whether the one True Light,

Kindle to Love, or Wrath—consume me quite,

One Glimpse of It within the Tavern caught

Better than in the Temple lost outright.

What! out of senseless Nothing to provoke

A conscious Something to resent the yoke

Of unpermitted Pleasure, under pain

Of Everlasting Penalties, if broke!

What! from his helpless Creature be repaid

Pure Gold for what he lent us dross-allay'd—

Sue for a Debt we never did contract,

And cannot answer—Oh the sorry trade!

LXX

Nay, but for terror of his wrathful Face,

I swear I will not call Injustice Grace;

Not one Good Fellow of the Tavern but

Would kick so poor a Coward from the place.

Oh Thou, who didst with pitfall and with gin

Beset the Road I was to wander in,

Thou wilt not with Predestin'd Evil round

Enmesh me, and impute my Fall to Sin?

Oh, Thou, who Man of baser Earth didst make,

And who with Eden didst devise the Snake;

For all the Sin wherewith the Face of Man

Is blacken'd, Man's Forgiveness give — and take!

Listen again. One Evening at the Close

Of Ramazan, ere the better Moon arose,

In that old Potter's Shop I stood alone

With the clay Population round in Rows.

And, strange to tell, among that Earthen Lot

Some could articulate, while others not:

And suddenly one more impatient cried—

"Who is the Potter, pray, and who the Pot?"

Then said another—"Surely not in vain

My Substance from the common Earth was ta'en,

That He who subtly wrought me into Shape

Should stamp me back to common Earth again."

LXXVI

Another said—"Why, ne'er a peevish Boy,

Would break the Bowl from which he drank in Joy;

Shall He that made the vessel in pure Love

And Fancy, in an after Rage destroy?"

LXXVII

None answer'd this; but after Silence spake

A Vessel of a more ungainly Make:

"They sneer at me for leaning all awry;

What! did the Hand then of the Potter shake?"

LXXVIII

"Why," said another, "Some there are who tell

Of one who threatens he will toss to Hell

The luckless Pots he marred in making—Pish!

He's a Good Fellow, and 'twill all be well."

Then said another with a long-drawn Sigh,

"My Clay with long oblivion is gone dry:

But, fill me with the old familiar Juice,

Methinks I might recover by-and-by!"

So while the Vessels one by one were speaking,

The Little Moon look'd in that all were seeking:

And then they jogg'd each other, "Brother! Brother!

Now for the Porter's shoulder-knot a-creaking!"

Ah, with the Grape my fading Life provide,

And wash my Body whence the Life has died,

And in a Windingsheet of Vine-leaf wrapt,

So bury me by some sweet Garden-side.

That ev'n my buried Ashes such a Snare

Of Perfume shall fling up into the Air,

As not a True Believer passing by

But shall be overtaken unaware.

Indeed the Idols I have loved so long

Have done my Credit in Men's Eye much wrong:

Have drown'd my Honour in a shallow Cup,

And sold my Reputation for a Song.

Indeed, indeed, Repentance oft before

I swore—but was I sober when I swore?

And then, and then came Spring, and Rose-in-hand

My thread-bare Penitence apieces tore.

And much as Wine has play'd the Infidel,

And robb'd me of my Robe of Honor—well,

I often wonder what the Vintners buy

One half so precious as the Goods they sell.

Alas, that Spring should vanish with the Rose!

That Youth's sweet-scented Manuscript should close!

The Nightingale that in the Branches sang,

Ah, whence, and whither flown again, who knows!

Would but the Desert of the Fountain yield

One glimpse—If dimly, yet indeed, reveal'd,

To which the fainting Traveller might spring,

As springs the trampled herbage of the field!

LXXXVIII

Ah Love! could thou and I with Fate conspire

To grasp this sorry Scheme of Things entire,

Would not we shatter it to bits—and then

Re-mould it nearer to the Heart's Desire!

Ah, Moon of my Delight who know'st no wane,

The Moon of Heav'n is rising once again:

How oft hereafter rising shall she look

Through this same Garden after me — in vain!

XC

And when like her, oh Saki, you shall pass

Among the Guests star-scatter'd on the Grass,

And in your joyous errand reach the spot

Where I made one — turn down an empty Glass!

TAMAM SHUD

GLOSSARY

BAHRAM GUR *(bah'-rām goor): Bahram of the Wild Ass,
Persian king and hunter.*

FERRASH *(fer-rāsh'): Servant, tent-pitcher.*

HATIM TAI *(hā'-tim tye): An Arab famed for generosity.*

IRAM *(ee' ram): A marvelous garden in Arabia.*

JAMSHYD *(jam'-sheed): Mythical Persian king supposed
to have reigned 700 years.*

KAIKHOSRU *(kye'-khos-roo): Mythical Persian king.*

KAIKOBAD *(kye'-ko-bād): Mythical Persian king.*

KUZA-NAMA *(koo'-za nā'-ma): Book of Pots.*

MAHMUD *(mah'-mood): Sultan Mahmud Ghasnaui, king
of Persia who was born in 969 A.D.*

MUEZZIN *(moo-ez'-zin): Mohammedan crier of the hour of
prayer.*

MUSHTARI *(mush'-ta-ree): The planet Jupiter.*

NAISHAPUR *(nay'-shā-poor): Naishapur, a city in Khora-
san, Iran, where Omar Khayyam was born.*

PARWIN *(par'-ween): A constellation, the Pleiades. Also a
feminine proper noun in Persian.*

PEHLEVI *(peh-'le-vee): Language of the Persians from the
third to the ninth centuries A.D.*

RAMAZAN *(ram-a-zān): Ninth month of the Mohammedan
year, devoted to fasting.*

RUBAYYAT *(roo'-bye-yằt): A stanza of four lines.*

RUSTUM *(rus'-tum): Mythical Persian hero.*

SAKI *(sa-kee): Cup bearer.*

TAMAM SHUD *(ta-mām' shood): The very end.*

Designed by Harald Peter.

Set in Linofilm Palatino, a 20th century typeface resembling a Venetian, designed by Hermann Zapf of Frankfurt.

Printed on Hallmark Eggshell Book paper.

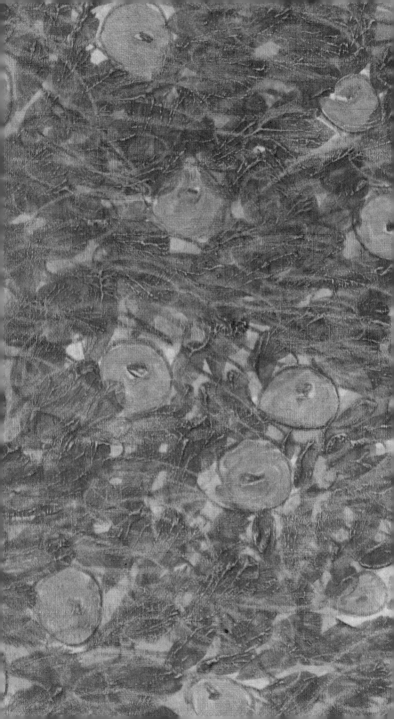